W9-BFW-661

CARS

Author:

Ian Graham was born in Belfast in 1953. He studied applied physics at The City University, London, and earned a postgraduate diploma in journalism, specializing in science and technology journalism. After four years as a magazine editor, he became a freelance author and journalist. Since then, he has written more than one hundred children's nonfiction books and numerous magazine articles.

Artist:

Mark Bergin was born in Hastings, England, in 1961. He studied at Eastbourne College of Art, and since 1983 he has specialized in historical reconstructions as well as aviation and maritime subjects. He lives in Bexhill-on-Sea with his wife and three children.

Consultant:

Monica Hughes is an experienced educational advisor and author of more than one hundred books for young children. She has been principal of a primary school, primary advisory teacher, and senior lecturer in early childhood education.

Editor:

Stephen Haynes

Editorial Assistant:

Mark Williams

This edition first published in 2014 by Book House

Distributed by Black Rabbit Books
P.O. Box 3263
Mankato
Minnesota MN 56002

© 2014 The Salariya Book Company Ltd

Printed in the United States of America.
Printed on paper from sustainable forests.

Cataloging-in-Publication Data is available from the Library of Congress

ISBN: 978-1-908973-94-8

CARS

Written by
IAN GRAHAM

Illustrated by
MARK BERGIN

Created and designed by
DAVID SALARIYA

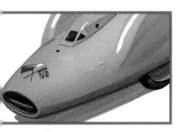

BOOK HOUSE
a SALARIYA *imprint*

Contents

The First Automobiles

The first "horseless carriages" were powered by steam. They were noisy, slow, and dirty. They were sometimes dangerous—the boilers could explode. The gasoline engine was invented in 1885. It made the car a much better form of transportation.

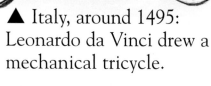

▲ Italy, around 1495: Leonardo da Vinci drew a mechanical tricycle.

◀ France, 1769: Nicolas-Joseph Cugnot's steam tractor reached 2.2 mph (3.6 km/h).

▼ England, 1826: Sir Goldsworthy Gurney built a steam carriage. These carriages had to stop about every 4 miles (6 km) to fill their boilers with water.

▲ Scotland, July 29, 1834: A steam carriage exploded. It was the first fatal motor accident.

Spark plug
Valve
Cylinder
Piston
Crankshaft

| 1 | 2 | 3 | 4 |

Fuel and air in | **Piston** moves up | **Spark plug** fires | Burnt gases out

▲ Most car engines work in four steps.

▲ Germany, 1885: Karl Benz built the first gasoline-powered car. It had three wheels and a one-cylinder engine. Its top speed was 9 mph (15 km/h).

▲ USA, 1908: The Ford Model T had a four-cylinder engine. It had a top speed of 40 mph (65 km/h). Its low price made it popular. More than 15 million cars of this type were sold.

▶ Germany, 1945: The Volkswagen "Beetle" became the most popular car ever built. More than 21 million were sold.

7

Designing a Car

Computers and robots make it quicker to design new cars. Computer animations show what the car will look like from all directions. Robots can be programmed to produce identical cars 24 hours a day.

▲ Most designs start with a sketch on paper.

▶ This drawing shows how much space is inside the car.

◀ Computer Aided Design (CAD) allows designers to check that all the parts fit and move properly.

▶ A computer-controlled machine makes a full-size mock-up out of clay or styrofoam.

COMPUTER MODELING

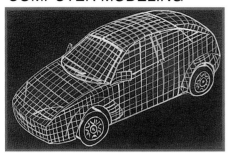

▲ This type of 3D drawing is called a "wireframe" image.

▲ Interior details are added to give this X-ray view.

▲ Color, texture, and shadows are added. This picture now looks like a photo of a real car.

▶ Cars are tested in a wind tunnel to see how air flows around them.

◀ A few **prototypes** are built by hand. These are driven on test tracks. Any problems can then be fixed.

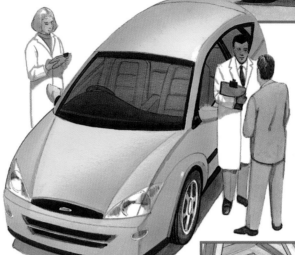

▶ Finally, the car goes into production. The steel body shell is welded by robots.

▼ More robots paint the car. Then the engine is put in and the wheels are fitted. The seats and windows are fitted last of all.

The Land Speed Record

▼ 1898: Count Gaston de Chasseloup-Laubat set the first land speed record of 39 mph (63 km/h).

Top speed: 230 mph (370 km/h)

▶ 1929: Henry Segrave's Golden Arrow

▼ 1931: Malcolm Campbell's Rolls-Royce-*powered* Blue Bird

Top speed: 246 mph (396 km/h)

Brake chute

Rear-wheel steering

Rolls-Royce Spey jet engines

Disk brakes

A new land speed record was set in 1997 in this sleek black jet-powered car called *Thrust SSC*. It had two 100,000-**horsepower** jet engines. These engines are normally used in fighter planes.

Thrust SSC blasts its way across the Black Rock Desert, Nevada. On October 15, 1997 it reached a record 763 mph (1,228 km/h). The Black Rock Desert is so big and flat that a car can **accelerate** to more than 600 mph (1,000 km/h). When *Thrust* SSC reached **supersonic** speed the spectators heard the telltale sonic boom.

Electric and steam-driven cars were the first to break land speed records. By the 1960s cars with jet engines could go even faster.

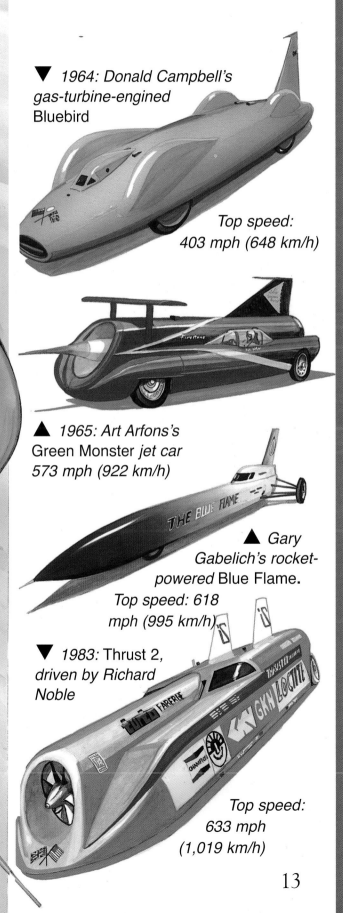

▼ *1964: Donald Campbell's gas-turbine-engined* Bluebird

Top speed: 403 mph (648 km/h)

▲ *1965: Art Arfons's* Green Monster *jet car 573 mph (922 km/h)*

▲ *Gary Gabelich's rocket-powered* Blue Flame*. Top speed: 618 mph (995 km/h)*

▼ *1983:* Thrust 2, *driven by Richard Noble*

Top speed: 633 mph (1,019 km/h)

13

Supercars & Muscle Cars

The fastest cars on the road are supercars and muscle cars.

◀ Chrysler Viper (USA)

8-liter, 10-cylinder engine; top speed 155 mph (250 km/h)

▼ Lamborghini Diablo VT (Italy)

5.7-liter, 12-cylinder engine; top speed more than 200 mph (320 km/h)

▼ Jaguar XJ220 (UK): 3.5-liter, 6-cylinder engine; top speed 217 mph (350 km/h)

Metal-coated,
electrically heated
windshield

Rising
doors

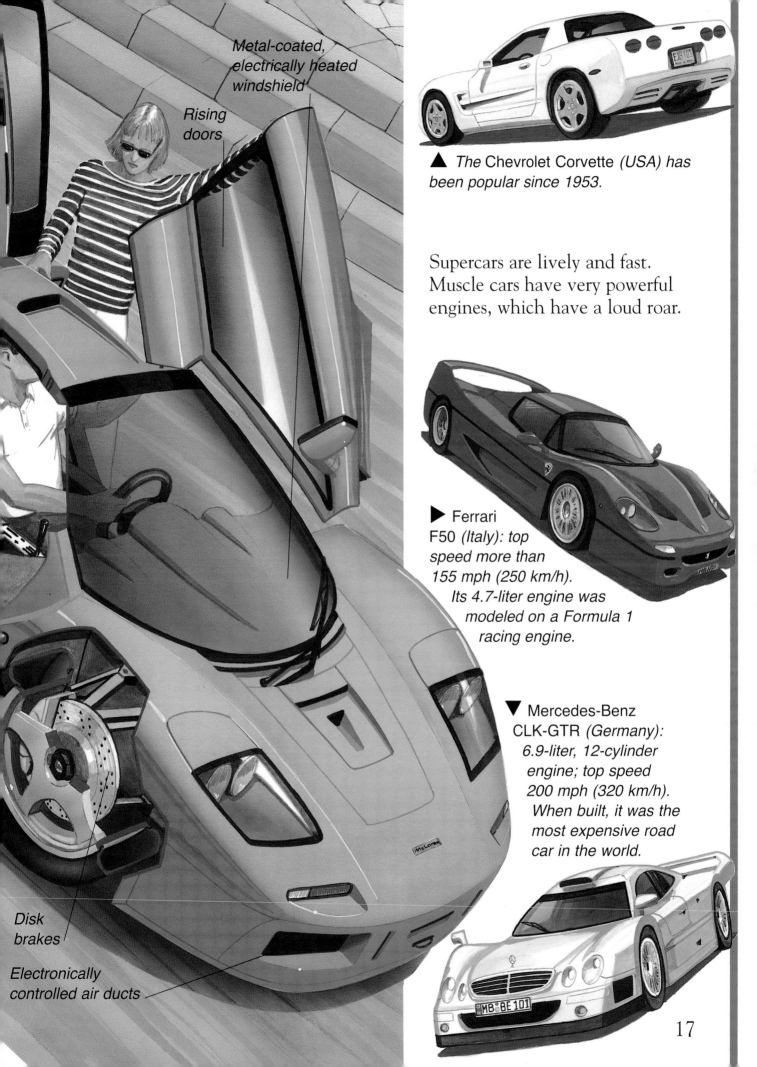

▲ *The* Chevrolet Corvette *(USA) has been popular since 1953.*

Supercars are lively and fast. Muscle cars have very powerful engines, which have a loud roar.

▶ Ferrari F50 *(Italy): top speed more than 155 mph (250 km/h). Its 4.7-liter engine was modeled on a Formula 1 racing engine.*

▼ Mercedes-Benz CLK-GTR *(Germany): 6.9-liter, 12-cylinder engine; top speed 200 mph (320 km/h). When built, it was the most expensive road car in the world.*

Disk brakes

Electronically controlled air ducts

17

Speed Kings

The kings of the race track are the single-seat racers. Their engines are at the back. The engines sit low between the wheels.

Dragster

▲ Dragsters are designed to go as fast as possible on a short, straight track. They have parachutes to help them stop.

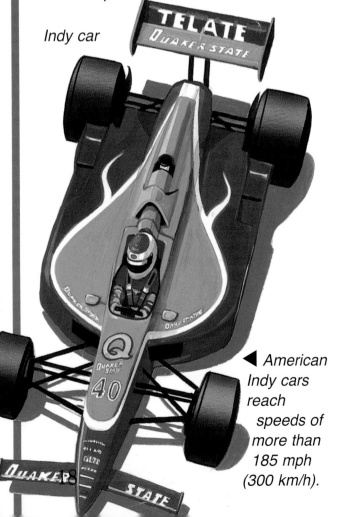

Indy car

◄ American Indy cars reach speeds of more than 185 mph (300 km/h).

Rear wing

Front wing

Fire-resistant suit
(in case of fuel spills)

Tire carrier

Tire changer

"Lollipop" stop–go sign

The pit crew crowds around a Formula 1 car during a **pit stop.** They change the wheels and refuel the car in 6 to 12 seconds.

Jack man

1950s

Juan Manuel Fangio

FORMULA 1 CHAMPIONS

Stirling Moss

1960s

Jim Clark

Jackie Stewart

1970s

Niki Lauda

1980s

Ayrton Senna

Alain Prost

1990s–2000s

Michael Schumacher

Sports Stars

Some racing cars are the same shape as ordinary cars. They are sometimes called "tin tops." Most races are won by the first car to cross the finish line.

Volvo S40

Porsche GTI

◀ The cars used in the British Touring Car Championship have an ordinary 2-liter engine. They run on unleaded gasoline.

▼ In the Le Mans 24-hour race, the winner is the car that goes the farthest in 24 hours. Three or more drivers take turns to drive the same car.

22

◀ Here, Jeff Burton and Jeff Gordon battle for the lead during the Daytona 500 motor race, which is held in February each year.

▼ Rally cars race against time, not each other. Each car sets off one minute after the car before. In stage rallies, the cars are driven at high speeds across forest tracks and rough ground. The navigator warns the driver of what is ahead.

Driver Carlos Sainz and navigator Luis Moya of Team Toyota Corolla

Sheer Luxury

L uxury cars like this Rolls-Royce Silver Seraph
are built to give a very
smooth, almost
silent ride.

▲ The
Cadillac DeVille
Concours has an electronic
"brain." The wipers
start automatically
when it rains.
The front seats
can give you a
massage!

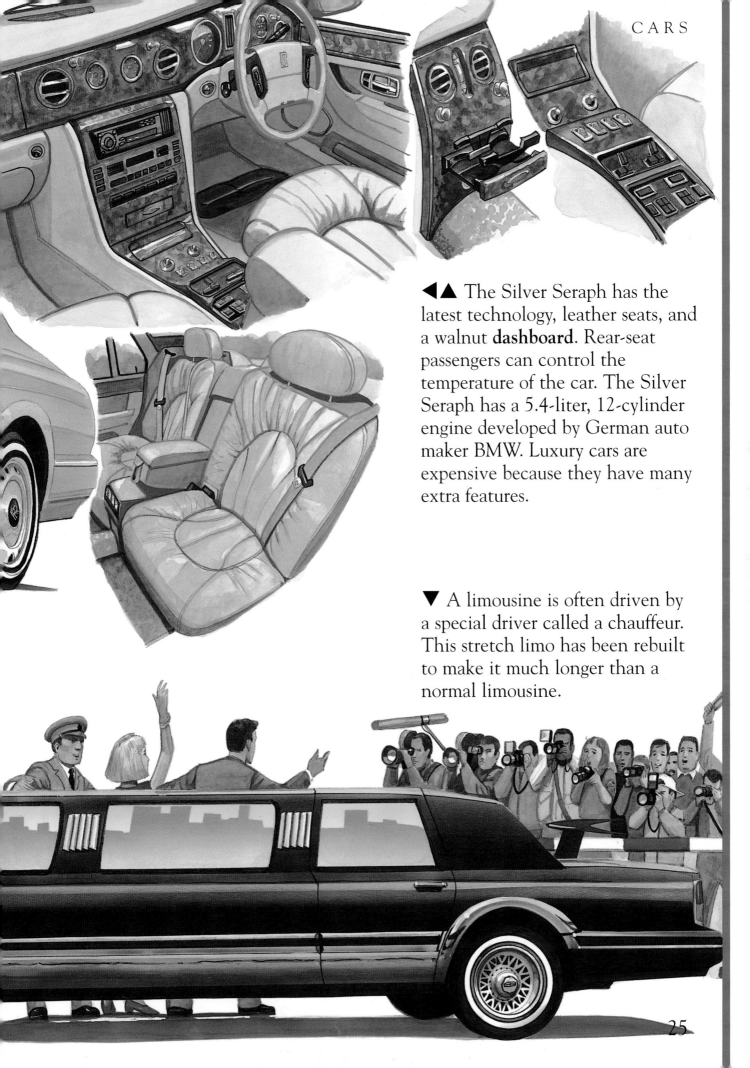

◄▲ The Silver Seraph has the latest technology, leather seats, and a walnut **dashboard**. Rear-seat passengers can control the temperature of the car. The Silver Seraph has a 5.4-liter, 12-cylinder engine developed by German auto maker BMW. Luxury cars are expensive because they have many extra features.

▼ A limousine is often driven by a special driver called a chauffeur. This stretch limo has been rebuilt to make it much longer than a normal limousine.

Car Safety

Headlights, anti-lock brakes, and eye-level brake lights help to prevent accidents. Seat belts and air bags protect passengers if an accident happens.

Safety-glass windshield

▲ In a crash test a car is deliberately crashed. Dummies show what would happen to real people in a car crash.

Brake lights warn ▶ people that a car is slowing down or stopping.

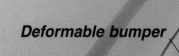

▲ The grooves in tires squeeze water out from under them. This stops the car skating over the water.

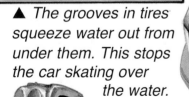

Anti-lock brakes stop the tires from losing grip and causing the car to skid.

Deformable bumper

Hazard light

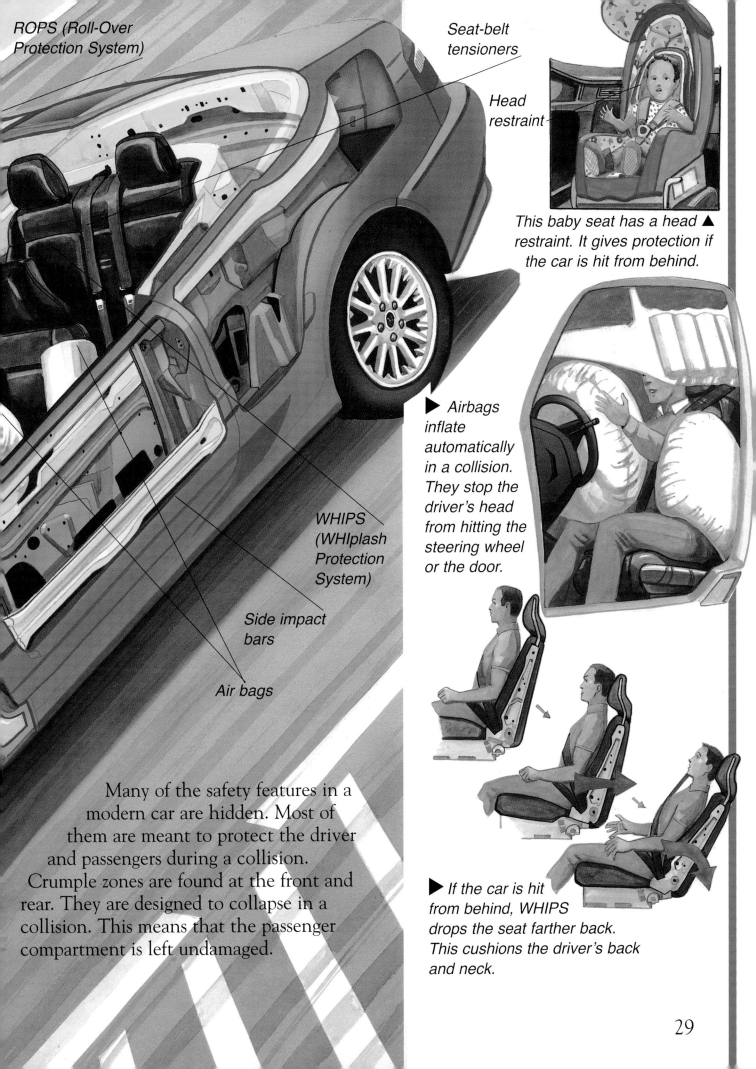

ROPS (Roll-Over Protection System)

Seat-belt tensioners

Head restraint

This baby seat has a head ▲ restraint. It gives protection if the car is hit from behind.

WHIPS (WHIplash Protection System)

Side impact bars

Air bags

▶ Airbags inflate automatically in a collision. They stop the driver's head from hitting the steering wheel or the door.

Many of the safety features in a modern car are hidden. Most of them are meant to protect the driver and passengers during a collision. Crumple zones are found at the front and rear. They are designed to collapse in a collision. This means that the passenger compartment is left undamaged.

▶ If the car is hit from behind, WHIPS drops the seat farther back. This cushions the driver's back and neck.

29

Useful Words

Accelerate
Go faster. The pedal a driver presses to make a car go faster is called the accelerator.

Carbon fiber
A strong, lightweight material made from very thin fibers of almost pure carbon.

Crankshaft
A kind of axle inside a gasoline or diesel engine, which is turned by the pistons as they move up and down. It is connected to the gears that drive the wheels.

Cylinder
A metal tube inside a car's engine, inside which the fuel is burned. Most car engines have four or more cylinders.

Dashboard
The control panel in front of a car's driver.

Deformable bumper
A bumper made from a soft material that changes shape when it touches something. It is safer than a hard metal bumper in accidents involving pedestrians or cyclists.

Disk brakes
Brakes that slow the car down by using hard, rough pads to grip a steel disk fixed to each road wheel.

Fuel
A liquid such as gasoline or diesel that is burned inside a car engine.

Horsepower
A measurement of the power of an engine.

Piston
A plunger that slides up and down inside an engine's cylinder, turning the crankshaft.

Pit stop
A visit to the pits (garages at the side of a motor-racing track) by a racing car during a race to have its tires changed and/or to fill up with fuel.

Pneumatic
Powered by air pressure.

Prototype
The first model of a car. It is tested to make sure that everything works properly before more cars are made.

Spark plug
A device that makes an electric spark to burn the fuel inside the cylinder and move the piston.

Supersonic
Faster than the speed of sound.

Valve
A device that allows fuel and air to flow into and out of a cylinder.

Milestones

1769 The first motor vehicle, a steam tractor, is built in France by Nicolas-Joseph Cugnot.

1885 Karl Benz builds the first gasoline-driven motor car.

1891 The first electric car, called the Electrobat, is built by Morris and Salom in Philadelphia, USA.

1893 Rudolf Diesel invents the diesel engine.

1895 André and Edouard Michelin make the first pneumatic (air-filled) tires for cars. They are based on John Boyd Dunlop's invention of the pneumatic tire.

1902 Disk brakes are invented for use in military vehicles.

1908 The Model T Ford goes into mass production in Detroit.

1911 The first self-starter for automobiles is invented. It replaces the starting handle.

1918 A third (yellow) light is added to red–green traffic lights.

1919 Hydraulic brakes (operated by oil pressure) are developed for automobiles.

1921 The first highway is built, in Germany.

1930 Cedric Dicksee develops a diesel engine for road vehicles.

1947 Raymond Loewy designs the first modern streamlined car, made by Studebaker.

1950 The Formula 1 World Motor Racing Championship begins.

1951 The US auto maker Chrysler fits its cars with power-assisted steering.

1953 A Jaguar car with disk brakes wins the Le Mans 24-hour race. This leads to the use of disk brakes in ordinary cars.

1961 The five-door car, or hatchback, is introduced by Renault.

1981 The air bag is invented by Daimler-Benz.

2008 At 23, British driver Lewis Hamilton becomes the youngest ever Formula 1 World Champion.

2008 US company Terrafugia reveals a prototype "roadable aircraft." This two-seater airplane can be converted into a car in just 15 seconds.

Index